Origin of a Name
1066

the story of Battle, Sussex

by
Michael Phillips

illustrated by Angus McBride

S.B. Publications

1066 England in Decline

EDWARD:REX

The Abbey and Town of Battle were the direct results of the greatest battle fought in England, the Battle of Senlac or Hastings. The Abbey was William the Conqueror's commemoration of his decisive victory, the Town arose naturally around the creation of the Abbey. But the Battle had more far-reaching consequences. It not only made possible the last conquest of England, it thereby infused a spirit which, with the Anglo-Saxon virtues, enabled the country to exert remarkable influence upon world history.

Early in 1066 the appearance of Halley's Comet was deemed an ill omen for England. Yet any south Saxon then present on the site of Battle could hardly imagine these gentle slopes soon becoming the scene of vicious conflict. In the realm of politics, however, there was already opposition to King Harold who had succeeded Edward the Confessor.

His kingdom, the Anglo-Saxon 'Empire', stable and advanced in government, was respected abroad. But it was disunited, withdrawing from the mainstream of European progress, its clergy criticised for sloth and ignorance. The Danish conquest, completed fifty years before, had been absorbed without dire upheaval by this people of like custom, heritage and language. England remained largely the England of the Anglo-Saxons, the England of ancient folklore, Alfred the Great and the Anglo-Saxon Chronicle.

The Norman Conquest did not so much revolutionise the ancient kingdom, it breathed a new dynamic into its organisation. The Normans of the eleventh century were the most able, adventurous race in Europe, a potent mixture of the Norse and French cultures. They were enjoying the rewards of initiative as the Anglo-Saxons had done in their Golden Age of the previous century. They were near the summit of their confidence, in need of outlets for an ambitious, restless energy.

In this period of insecurity, when leaders of action predominated, they were breeding a succession of such men, headed by William, Duke of Normandy. But England, unsure of its destiny after the collapse of Canute's empire*, produced only one leader of similar calibre. King Harold alone stood between Anglo-Saxon England and the imposing of a harsher, more disciplined regime upon the country. He alone could overcome the terrifying forces combining against his kingdom.

Yet the issue of the struggle between England and Normandy was far from certain; the decision of the Battle long in doubt.

* Canute reigned over England, Denmark and Norway.

The English Succession

Edward the Confessor being childless, an uncertain succession provoked the lust for power and adventure symbolic of the era. Harold's family, the ambitious Godwins, had built up extensive dominions from humble beginnings. By the eve of the Norman Conquest they had achieved the climax of their ambition with the crowning of Harold. But Tostig Godwinson, expelled from his earldom of Northumbria, and envious of the King, his brother, conspired abroad to recover his authority and promote a foreigner to power. Tostig's desires linked naturally with the ambitions of William of Normandy and Harald Hardrada, King of Norway. With three great leaders ready to risk everything for England, a revengeful traitor in the wings, the scene was set for high drama.

Having established himself over his feuding nobility, William was looking for the supreme challenge. He had won concessions of the crown from his cousin, King Edward, and Harold himself, the Earl of Wessex and Edward's counsellor. Harold's concession was the more binding, for he had solemnly sworn over holy relics to acknowledge William on the death of the Confessor. How could Harold*, a contender for the throne in his own right, have agreed to become Duke William's man?

* See "Harold and His England", the companion to this booklet.

Harold

4

Hardrada

In 1064 he had been cast ashore from shipwreck close to Normandy and fallen into William's hands. The Duke and his hostage had kept company, fought alongside in Brittany, hunted and feasted together. Each respected the other with William, the dominating character, extracting his ransom for the Earl's freedom.

The third claimant to England, Harald Hardrada, was a mighty warrior in the Viking tradition. Tales of his deeds resounded through the royal halls of Christendom from the Eastern Empire of Byzantium to the English capital of Winchester and the growing metropolis of London. His reputation as a soldier was greatest at this stage of the drama.

William

Preparations for War

The English army. The Housecarle, a well-armed and well-paid professional, fanatically loyal. Mailcoat, sword, spears, shield and axe, nasal-helmeted. Rode to battle but usually fought on foot.
Left, select fyrdsman, recruited and paid for by town or village which also supplied food and arms.
Right, general fyrdsman, recruited only in emergency. Every able-bodied man brought straight from farm and plough, armed with makeshift weapons.

When he was crowned in the pious Edward's new West Minster in January, 1066, Harold of England realised he would have to defend his authority. Even in England this authority was questioned. His own folk of the south (Wessex) and East Anglia readily accepted him, but those of the north gave him only grudging respect. The motives of the Godwins had long been suspect and Harold had broken his sacred oath to acknowledge William his sovereign. With his crown precarious he did everything possible to establish himself. He made a royal progress of conciliation northwards. He sacrificed his mistress Edith Swanneck, the mother of his children, and married Eadgyth, sister of the northern Earls. He had a quantity of coins minted and circulated, embossed 'Haroldus Rex Anglorum'.

Norman Knight on heavy charger and wearing chain armour with reinforced chest piece. Armed with sword and light lance, hurled overhead or used for stabbing. Men-at-arms mail clad and well-armed, archer from Brittany.

He was confident in himself and England's defences, and seemed to have every prospect of overcoming each menace separately. From May to September, he maintained the Fyrd (territorial army) and the fleet in readiness on the south coast. He knew the Normans, driven by William's ambition and indignation, were bound to attempt an invasion. In fact, they had a formidable task if they were to do so in the year 1066. This was to be no mere plunder raid but a fully-organised conquest of a still-powerful kingdom.

First William determined to gain the Pope's blessing and support. He proclaimed his invasion a crusade against Harold, the perjurer and usurper, rather than an attack upon England. Harold had not only broken his most sacred oath of allegiance, he had had himself elected by a minority of his peers. (Harold was elected by the Witanagemot or Meeting of Wise Men. This was not unknown but there were some absentees with the election soon after Christmas.) The Pope's support gained by one means and another, William was able to persuade his followers to join whole-heartedly in the enterprise. Though many were motivated by plunder, the fighting of a religious war appealed to their superstitions.

William had to construct a fleet of some 500-700 vessels to transport not simply soldiers, but horses and prefabricated castles, across the Channel. He regarded the use of cavalry essential against the English Housecarles (royal guards), possibly the best infantry in Europe. He also realised that wooden castles would be necessary strongholds against a rebellious population. The Bayeux Tapestry shows the labours of shipwrights and carpenters building the armada during the spring and summer.

The Norman Ships were based on the Viking pattern – shallow draught, clinker-built and flexible. They were equipped for rowing or sailing with a square rigged sail of heavy striped linen.
Here the finishing touches are being put to William's Command Ship, the 'Mora', presented to him by his wife Matilda.
There were about 14 men (apart from the crew) and 4 horses to each ship – arms, provisions and building materials as well.

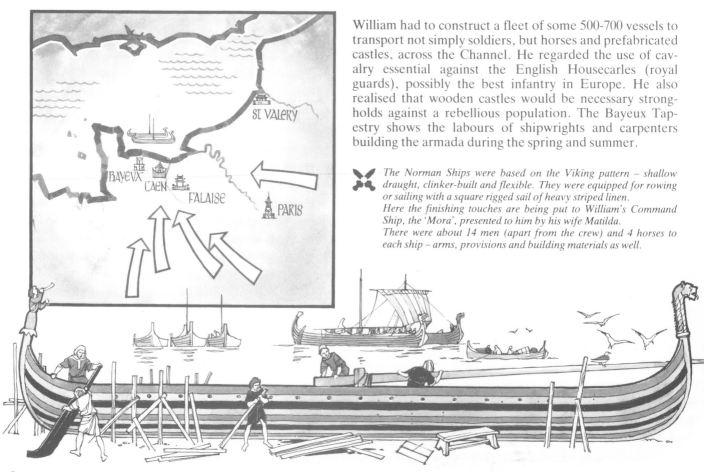

Meanwhile, he was training and assembling an interprovincial army, for he had to boost the Norman majority with foreign auxiliaries. He combined his forces and completed preparations within a few months – proof enough of his extraordinary ability and energy.

But when all was ready anti-climax struck. Adverse winds prevented the armada from setting forth on the expedition. It was as if Providence itself was their ally for, if they had invaded immediately, the English fleet and army could have defeated them piecemeal. Now, with autumn approaching, no landing likely and the harvest to be gathered and celebrated, Harold dispersed his forces. He had committed them rather too early, but he too had displayed extraordinary energy and ability.

Anything could happen before the final curtain.

 The winds which confined William's fleet to port enabled Harald Hardrada's warships to cross the North Sea and invade Northumbria.

North and South Invaded

The adverse winds which postponed the Norman invasion made that of the Norsemen possible. Under the legendary Harald Hardrada and the traitor Tostig, they defeated the English under Earls Edwin and Morcar in Northumbria soon after landing. Aware of his duty, of the dangers of waiting, Harold of England reacted immediately. With characteristic vigour he rode north at the head of his Housecarles, collecting levies of the Fyrd en route. Making rapid progress by forced marches, he surprised the invaders at Stamford Bridge, near York, on September 25th. He rode forward to parley with Tostig but, failing to win him over, led his orthodox phalanx of infantry to the attack.

After overcoming a giant defender of the bridge, crossing the river Derwent and repeated assaults by the Housecarles, Harold gained one of the bloodiest victories of the Middle Ages. Not only were Hardrada and Tostig both killed, the remaining Vikings needed a mere 24 of their 300 long ships to return to Norway. The rout had been followed by hunting down and savage slaughter — Harold of England had completed his victory.

Providence now played as false a stroke as any general has suffered in the history of war. While Harold was recovering with his army in York, the wounded being tended, the slain buried, an exhausted rider brought news that the Normans had invaded. At the appropriate moment the winds had veered in their favour. They had crossed the Channel from St. Valery-sur-Somme* with William's command ship outdistancing the fleet at first, but otherwise in good order. They had waded ashore unopposed at Pevensey, manhandling mighty castles and fiery chargers. They were already erecting a fortress, the cavalry were ravaging the Sussex countryside with impunity.

* Twin town of Battle.

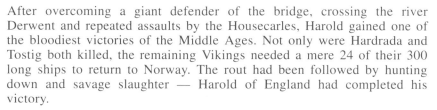

Tradition says that Harold was feasting when the messenger burst in.

It was a calculated act to draw Harold south to repulse this
second threat to his kingdom and avenge the family earldom. Though his army was seriously reduced, he retraced
his route south with renewed speed and vigour. Some of
the warriors who continued to ride or march in his wake
fell by the wayside or failed to keep pace. Others who had

arrived late for the march north partly made up the losses. Aware of the need for reinforcements, reforming and consulting, Harold waited about six days in London. Due to poor communications and disunity, he was unable to gather an army representing his kingdom, yet again he pressed south. Still confident, anxious to stop the devastation, avenge his Sussex folk and for God to declare him in the right, he pounded along the Downland tracks, hewed his way through the Wealden forest to repeat his northern victory. A swelling body of southern Fyrdsmen rode and strode as best they could to maintain the furious progress.

The march of Harold's army from York to London in a week or less was a remarkable achievement. Not only were the soldiers battle-weary but they had to live off villages and farmlands they passed through. Those who collapsed by the wayside were taken care of – or robbed – by the people of the area.

Historians have been fulsome in their criticism of Harold's course of action. He should have waited for a greater army, for time to recover before confronting William. He should have laid waste the south-east, starved William into submission or destroyed him through inaction. He should have accepted his brother Gyrth's noble offer to lead the army, not risked his life and kingdom .... But are these strategists able to understand the logistics, the compulsions of this distant period?

William had established his headquarters at Hastings and erected a temporary fortress there. Continuing to ravage and pillage, he was hoping the reaction would soon reach him. His hopes were fulfilled sooner than he had hoped. Late on the 13th October, his outposts sent gallopers warning of the enemy's headlong advance. The straggling masses of the Fyrd, trotting, cantering, half-running, half-walking – their torches aflame in the darkness, they were hardly difficult to foresee. But King Harold was still intent upon surprise. Late on the 13th, early on the 14th he was collecting his forces by the Hoar Apple Tree. He was preparing to drive this second host of invaders into the sea.

There was not so much as a hamlet at Battle then, though the southern slopes of the Town were cultivated. Even so this well-known landmark commanded the approaches to the port of Hastings, William's base. The site of the Hoar Apple Tree is a matter of dispute. Most authorities place it on Caldbec Hill (at the top of Mount Street, then the London Road) with its fine views towards Telham Hill and the Norman outposts. Today, its white windmill at the summit, it remains a conspicuous hilltop for miles around.

One local authority on the Battle preferred another high point, the Watch Oak (until recently Rother Council offices, now flats).

14

c	Caldbec Hill
h	Harold's Command Post and Abbey
w	William's Command Post
1.	Watch Oak
2.	Mount St.
3.	High St.
4.	Upper Lake
5.	Abbey Gateway
6.	St. Mary's Church
7.	To Telham Hill
8.	Malfosse
9.	Whatlington Rd.

 Foot Soldiers

 Cavalry

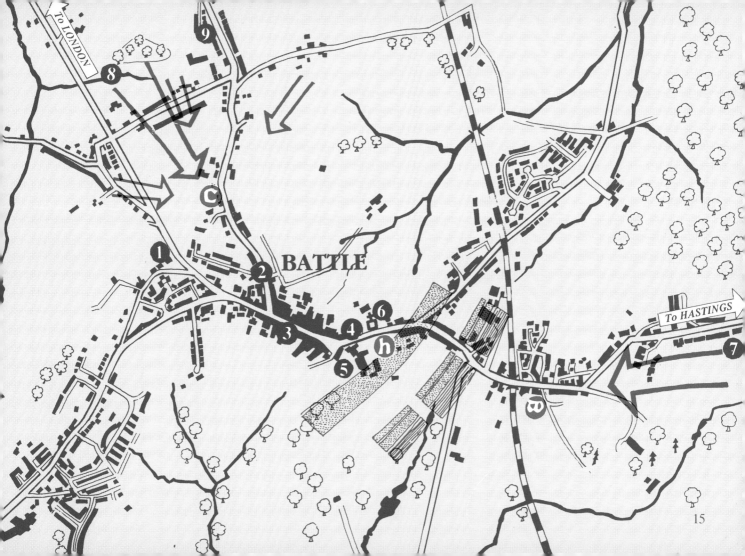

To LONDON

BATTLE

To HASTINGS

15

In either case Harold had chosen an excellent position from which to deploy. He had, however, lost the advantage of surprise. Seeing the Norman army appearing on Telham heights soon after daybreak on the 14th, he hastily stationed his men to block their advance. He drew them up below Caldbec Hill, on the ridge facing south and guarding the route to London, what the Normans later called Santlache (Senlac). He established his command post, his glittering standard of the 'Fighting Man' and the 'Dragon of Wessex', where the High Altar of Battle Abbey was to stand. About fifty yards below and three hundred to east and west either side, nearly rectangular with the High Street, his army awaited the onslaught closepacked. To the rear, on the edge of the forest, the ponies which had brought them were herded, tethered or roamed loose. The camp followers gathered around the embers of the camp fires – rumour-mongering, predicting.

In the front ranks, their Nordic locks flowing, the House-carles stood sturdy and intent as their Waterloo successors, the 'Thin Red Line'. Behind and around them, ten to twelve ranks deep, the Fyrd and motley levies milled, stamped, cursed and scorned the invaders. Their enemies answered with Frenchified insults, sneers of contempt for the currish defenders. The yelling of orders, clanking of arms, the braying of horns, neighing of horses accompanied the discordant prelude to battle. An inconstant trickle of Fyrdsmen and half-armed peasants swelled the English numbers from the outlying districts. Some, finding themselves too cramped, deserted in protest soon after arrival.

Herein lay the chief danger to the Anglo-Saxons – the masses of Fyrd and peasantry who had come to save their families and homesteads from further rapine and pillage. It was not that they lacked courage or arms, though the peasants' weapons were crude and bows and arrows almost non-existent. In leathern jackets and caps, the Fyrd had enough spears, javelins, bill hooks, scythes, stone-headed axes (for hurling) and rounded shields to withstand the impending assaults – provided they kept their

formation. Success in fact depended upon discipline, upon whether in the heat and turmoil of battle, they could resist the temptation to leave the line to fight as individuals.

Of the Housecarles' prowess and discipline there was no doubt. Nasal-helmeted, chain-mailed like the majority of the enemy, protected by long triangular shields, wielding heavy axes, hurling javelins, they alone could hold the English together. Harold circulated orders through his thegns (warrior nobility) that the formation on the ridge must be retained at all costs. That they must stand their ground and demoralise the Normans before counter-attacking. But what were battle orders against a lifetime of excess in moments of joy triumphant.

As the opposing forces stood to arms against a countryside of autumn colour, their helmets glinting, banners waving, they looked remarkably equal.

The Battle

The Battle took a course predictable to historians and half-predictable to Harold. A Godfearing man, the founder of Waltham Abbey, he was troubled with foreboding as he perceived the situation of Stamford Bridge reversing itself. Witnessing the invaders' descent into the valley below, William's papal banner borne aloft, his breach of the holy oath was hellishly remembered; it nagged at his confidence. Conscience, the strains of a brief but exacting reign, the exertions of the campaign were having their reaction upon this middle-aged general. The authority he had previously displayed was not so evident here. The struggle he was to put up was noble, heroic yet from the onset near-desperate.

William was several years younger, fresher, physically more substantial – a great commander at the peak of his power. This exhortation* to his men before the Battle

* Taken from Robert Wace's poem of 1160. Romanticised doubtless but a good brief psychology of William the General.

18

shows his determination, intelligence and persuasion: 'For God's sake spare not … strike hard at the beginning; don't stop to take spoil; all the booty shall be in common … plenty for everyone. There will be no safety in asking quarter or in flight; the English will never love or spare a Norman. Felons they were and felons they are; false they were and false they will be … Neither the coward running well, nor the bold man smiting well, will be the better liked by the English … You may fly to the sea, but no further … the English will overtake you and slay you in your shame … Therefore, since flight will not save you, fight and you will conquer. I have no doubt of the victory …'

His army assembled in three main divisions. By far the largest, the Normans, was in the centre, their Breton allies to the left (west), the French and Flemings to the right (east). The Battle began with low-angled volleys of arrows from the Norman archers at about a hundred yards range. The English reply of javelins, stone-headed axes and other missiles was reserved for closer quarters. Their ar-rows exhausted, mainly wasted on the shields of the Housecarles, the Norman infantry made a series of attacks uphill against the English missilry, the ridge defenders.

The fighting was now fully joined. War cries of "Out! Out!" from the English and "Dex Aide!" ("God help us!") from the invaders surrendered to the clash and clangour of arms. Screams of agony, the yelling of abuse, the fleeting appeal for mercy resounded through the valley, echoing around. Again and again the men-at-arms struggled upwards only to be repulsed, scores of them falling beneath the axe-wielding Housecarles, the Fyrd fighting manfully alongside. Numbers of dead, dying and wounded began to mar the hillside with grey, brown and gore, as the cavalry were committed. Not having developed the charge en masse which might have broken the English, they galloped uphill in groups. They lunged or hurled their spears, cut and slashed with their swords, but the phalanx was inpenetrable, shielded, bristling with steel. The unearthly whinnying of wounded and terrified steeds mingled with the crescendo of battle. The cavalry too were repeatedly driven downhill, the position of the invaders seemed hopeless. Individuals then groups, mainly on the Breton wing, started fleeing the scene in terror. Footsoldiers were trampled underhoof, underfoot or swept aside in this anguished career for safety. Threatening, impious roaring from Bishop Odo, William's half-brother, failed to stem incipient panic.

Then with the instinct of genius, he turned his horsemen against the hordes of English tearing downhill in hectic pursuit. In the valley, his knights, regrouped, were soon able to thrust and cut their way through the scattered bodies, the helpless individuals of the heedless Fyrd. Only on a hillock* behind the Breton lines did a collection of them put up strong resistance against the savage counter-attacks of the cavalry. From this moment, through the jeering and enticement of their foes, through sheer weariness, still heedless of commands from above, Fyrdsmen continued to sally forth. Singly, in small bodies they strode out to avenge and prove themselves. Their end was inevitable.

* This is just south of Battle Abbey School playing fields.

To many of the Fyrd, impatient after continuous attack, confined to the ridge for long enough, this was joy triumphant. Their pent-up animal spirits cried out for bloody revenge and total victory. But the moment of crisis brought William himself charging into the valley from his command post opposite Harold's standards. Amid the uproar of confusion and disaster, he was livid to hear the rumour of his own death. Raising his helmet, standing in his stirrups to deny it, he bellowed his presence, pointed to the papal banner then towards the perjurer. He insisted still upon victory, he bullied and rallied his fleeing troops into some sort of order.

A respite around midday was used by William to reform his forces, by Harold to shorten his lines. Encouragements were passed, crude jests made, deeds boasted, slain comrades pitied. Scraps of bread, meat and fowl, palmfuls of corn were devoured. Water was sloshed and scooped from marshy streams* near the invaders' position, from woodland streams to the English right — the calls of nature answered. The wounded were succoured, the dead men and horses dragged clear for the next charge up the ridge.

For a while after the renewal, separate assaults by cavalry and infantry failed to break the defenders' formation. Yet the English were suffering increasingly from declining numbers and fatigue. Their line began to waver, to cave in here and there as breaches were made then, urged on from behind they closed it again. The assaults persisted, they could no longer hold position. Their line irreparably breached now, they gave ground. Gradually, painfully, individually they retreated — upward. A thegn, weary of the slaughter, was speared through, the blood spurting, grey mail discolouring. A Housecarle struggled manfully to drag a Norman knight from his charger — to confront him on even terms. Another, wielding his axe overhead, had stripped to the waist in the heat and turmoil of infighting. Harold himself, praying for retreat by night, rested on his axe handle, aching, perspiring.

Perceiving the English had lost the advantages of height, formation and numbers, William ordered an assault of his three arms. As in the morning the attack was heralded by volleys of arrows; fresh shafts had been brought by wag-gon from Beauport Park (on the Battle to Hastings road). This time they were shot high into the air to hail upon the heads of the English. As some defenders shielded their faces, it appears King Harold continued to ply his axe and was half-blinded by the legendary arrow — the terrible frustration, the lingering agony. However, contemporary chroniclers often dramatised a great warrior's death by attributing it to a shaft piercing his throat or an eye. In any event, Harold was wounded and survived the final barrage to die with his thegns and Housecarles, overwhelmed by the combined assault. The Bayeux Tapestry shows that he met his end at the hands of Norman knights who had constantly sought him out.

* These still exist — see map.

21

The desperate struggle for the English standards and headquarters was over by early evening. The declining sunset — a suffusion of red, pink and mauve over the Downs to the west — seemed to symbolise a declining England. The English were leaderless, the King mutilated by the knights he had thwarted, his two brothers slaughtered earlier in the Battle. But it was a noble end, an end worthy of England, as was the final stand of the Housecarles. They refused to surrender and were fought or trampled to death, almost to the last man.

The survivors fled under cover of darkness to join bodies of the Fyrd who had escaped to the edge of the forest. Here a fierce rearguard action was waged. Bands of pursuing horsemen careering over Caldbec Hill came upon a miniature ravine, later named Malfosse.* Unable to rein back, their steeds snorting, neighing shrilly with fear of the unknown, riders and steeds fell headlong to their deaths. In the forest redoubt the other side, the English fought the resistance of despair, and drove back their adversaries. Only organised charges forced them to succumb and retreat further into the deep wooded mystery behind.

William called off the pursuit and established his headquarters amid the carnage where Harold had died. Here a day or two later came Edith Swan-neck, his mistress, and Gytha, the tragic mother of four Godwins killed in three weeks of battles. She was permitted by an arrogant victor

* Identifiable as the watercourse flowing down westwards from Oak Wood — see map.

to take her son's body and bury it by the Hastings shore he had so vainly defended. Here too came humbler lovers and looters to search in grief, greed and revulsion whatever they sought. And here on the brink of conquest, William is said to have remembered the vow he had made before the Battle, that he might be granted the victory: 'that upon this place of battle I will found a suitable free Monastery, for the salvation of you all, and especially of those who fall*; and this I will do in honour of God and his saints.'

As the Conqueror created the embryo of a nation, his Abbey of Battle was born.

* Special services are still held for the fallen in the Battle parish church of St. Mary the Virgin.

The King's Abbey

William had to subdue the still-hostile English, particularly in the north. While he harried them to death and scarred the face of the earth between York and Durham, he could not attend to his monastery. However, when he was reminded of his vow, his conscience was pricked and he entrusted the monk William Faber with its foundation. At first there were complaints about the site being unsuitable, stone being difficult to obtain and the shortage of water. But King William was determined to build upon the site where he had won his crown, and he told Faber and his brethren to spare no expense: '... I shall so amply provide for this place that wine shall be more abundant here than water ...' Beautiful stone was transported from Normandy, shipped as tradition has it up the river Brede, carted to Battle and the work begun.

After further delays, the building was sufficiently advanced by 1076 for the first Abbot, Gausbert, to be blessed by the Bishop of Chichester at the high altar. Already King William had ambitious plans for his abbey; 'he had intended to make it for greatness and wealth, one of the principal monasteries in England'. He endowed it richly and expected not only to attend the dedication with his old comrades-in-arms, but to be buried here. He died, however, after campaigning in France and was laid to rest in Caen. The dedication was postponed but the Conqueror had so impressed upon his son, William Rufus, the significance of the Abbey that he attended to his father's wish as if his soul depended on it.

Building methods taken from somewhat later building of St. Alban's Cathedral but unlikely to have been much different. 'Crane', scaffolding and ladders from near-contemporary manuscript illuminations.
Barrow from French illumination. Style of column etc. from Monks' 'Common Room' Battle.

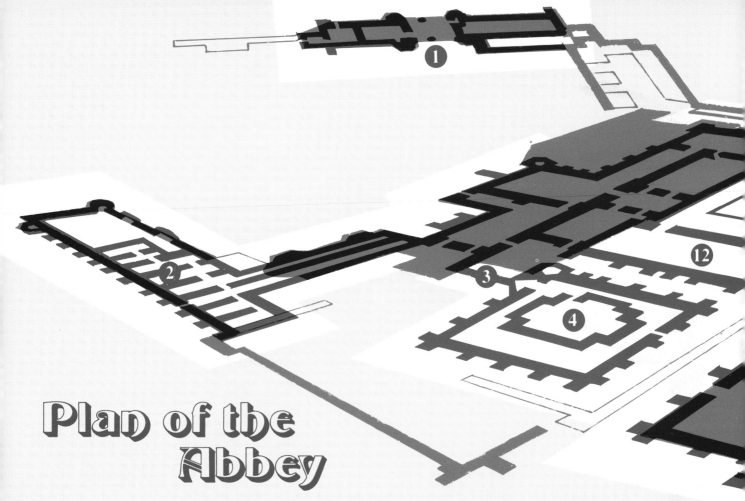

Plan of the Abbey

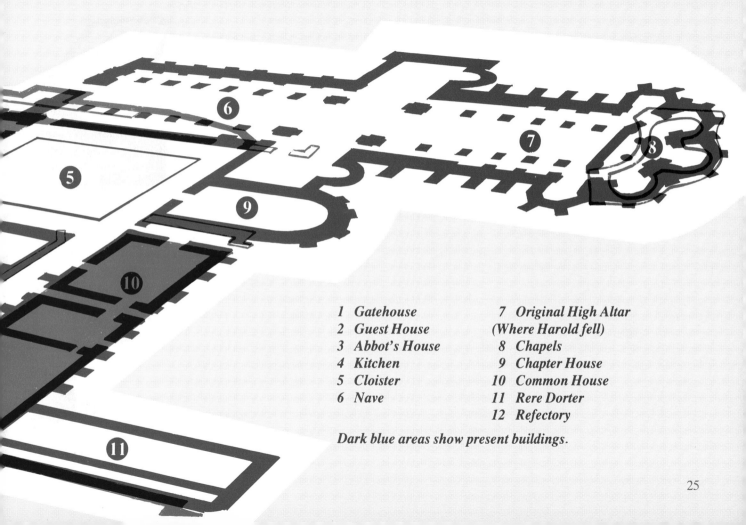

1 Gatehouse
2 Guest House
3 Abbot's House
4 Kitchen
5 Cloister
6 Nave

7 Original High Altar
(Where Harold fell)
8 Chapels
9 Chapter House
10 Common House
11 Rere Dorter
12 Refectory

Dark blue areas show present buildings.

On February 11th, 1094, he came to Battle 'in great splendour with an innumerable train of barons and the common people', and seven bishops. He was received by Anselm, the Archbishop of Canterbury, with a concourse of the clergy 'whom he caused to dedicate the Abbey with great pomp'. Imagine the fiery Rufus in his crown, the heraldic surcoats of his barons, the gold embroidered cassocks of the bishops, the duller cassocks of the clergy, the brown jerkins of the labourers, the rude hovels of the first community below. They assemble as near the altar as rank permits, the common folk crushing and peering outside the Church. A few old warriors relive the struggle here almost thirty years before.

The original Abbey Church was not big and the monastic buildings were simple, but from the late 12th to the 14th century Battle Abbey grew in magnificence to become one of the great religious houses. Its exceptional privileges, rich endowments of land and treasures, the flow of gifts from those under its influence gave it an honourable position in the new kingdom.

It is necessary to realise that this is a description of the Abbey as it existed. The Abbot's dwelling, the Gatehouse, the shell of the Dormitory and buildings beneath it remain, but the Benedictine Abbey of St. Martin 'de Bello' was destroyed in 1538. To get an idea of the Abbey before this date, visualize coming through the Gateway upon its medieval splendour.

On the left is the great Minster. Next to this is the Abbot's house with its private chapel. In the great hall or his private apartments he receives royalty, nobles, prelates and merchants of substance. In the outer Courtyard are the stables and stores. The inner courtyard, the Cloister, is the life centre of the Abbey. To the north is the enlarged Church and near the original High Altar (and the Battle memorial) lies the crypt in a hollow. East of the Cloister is the Chapter House where the monks meet daily, south of it the Refectory where they eat their meals to Latin readings of the lives of the saints. On the south-east corner of the Chapter House is the Slype, a passage with stone benches for the monks to receive visitors under supervision. To the south of the Slype is the dormitory or Dorter, above a room warmed by braziers, the Novices' chamber and the library or Scriptorium. Here are fine pillars of Purbeck marble and the white stones imported from Normandy are clearly visible.

East of this are the Prior's quarters and the Infirmary, where the monks are bled periodically and the elder brethren live in retirement. One of the Prior's duties is to visit the Infirmary to make sure there are no malingerers. Near the Infirmary are the water closets, the Reredorter, flushed by a spring which rises higher up the slope. Underneath the Abbey is an extensive system of drains, legendary secret passages; and under the Guest house (the terrace) are the Cellarer's office and his store houses.

In the centre of this religious complex is the Bell Tower. Its four bells toll the Gospel of eternal life to the brethren and townsfolk. The resonance is borne across the fields, through the dales and over the hills.

Abbey Rights Defended

Amongst the Abbey privileges, one of the most unusual was the Abbot's absolute power over the lands within one and a half miles of his monastery. In this leuga or lowey he administered justice, his tenants owed only him service and he himself was independent of the Bishop. He was also a mitred abbot and from 1295 to the Dissolution was summoned as a peer to Parliament.

Various Bishops of Chichester not unnaturally disputed this authority. The most persistent was Hilary, who was resisted with equal persistence by the influential Abbot Walter (elected 1139). The Bishop reported the Abbot's stubbornness to the Pope, who instructed Walter to 'obey faithfully his bishop and master'. The Abbot appealed to the Crown and the matter came before Henry II. With the support of the King, who saw his prerogative threatened, and Thomas à Becket, then his Chancellor, the case was decided in the Abbot's favour and the Abbey Charters confirmed.

Witness the venerable Walter after decades of struggle for Abbey rights. He has been visiting one of the many abbatial churches and is now so frail he has to be drawn back to Battle in a litter.

There he is laid on a sackcloth and ashes in the Chapter House. The brethren surround him, chanting devotedly, monotonously for the departing spirit.

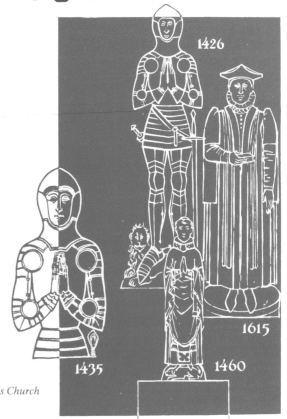

Brasses in St. Mary's Church

A Prosperous Township

As the Abbey grew in influence the Township of Battle prospered. The descendants of the labourers who had built the monastery benefited from its trade, from the nobility and clergy who paid their respects, from the reputation of such saintly abbots as Odo (1175). By the time of Abbot Walter Battle was the market centre of the area, its goods and trade supervised by guilds*. The Abbot had the right to levy tolls on cattle tethered, and booths erected, on Market Green (the car park outside the Gateway).

Henry I had given permission for a three-day fair in July, and later another was held, appropriately, at St. Martinstide (11th November). These became events for the traders and labourers, the jesters and jugglers, the harlots and the ale houses. From the early days there were inns which thrived during the Charter Fairs. They included 'The Bull' (site of the present Bull Inn, 27 High Street), and 'The Cow' next door. The Charter Fairs gave way to Pleasure and Cattle Fairs, the former continuing until 1938, the latter until more recently — 1967. The Green where much of the marketing took place gradually became cobbled over, through the bull ring in the centre serves as a reminder.

* There were guild halls at Claverham, covering west Battle, and Sandlake, covering the east.
References: "Bygone Battle" and "Lordship and Community".

The early dwellings along the High Street and Mount Street were mainly of wooden planks or logs with earthen floors. The streets were rough and rutted ways for horse-drawn waggons, litters and cattle, monastic processions and humble peasants alike. The peasants were not always humble. Later in the Middle Ages they began to voice their discontents with feudal service and low wages, their jealousy of the Abbey was aroused. Occasionally a clever local lad was raised by monkish scholarship, even sent on a grant to Oxford. And more romantically, the fair looks of some Saxon lass could surpass her home-spun, give her a life undreamed of with some visiting merchant, prelate or noble.

During the Hundred Years' War at least two abbots set aside the pastoral staff to repel French invaders. One of them, Alan de Ketling (1324), was allowed to fortify the Abbey by Edward III, who also set a precedent by not visiting the royal foundation. It was Abbot Alan who built the fine Gateway that still dominates Battle. He died of the Black Death which caused much distress in Abbey and Town.

In 1377 the French took over the Isle of Wight and captured the Prior of Lewes. They sailed on to Winchelsea but Abbot Hamo de Offington raised his ten-

The Abbey Gateway in the 19th Century.

The Warrior Abbot

ants and, donning his armour, marched them to the defence of the town. Sword in hand, his commands ringing above the din of the siege, he was more like some gallant knight than the Father of a revered abbey. After a lusty defence, the French were driven off and he became the hero of a local proverb: "Ware the Abbot of Battle, when the Prior of Lewes is taken prisoner".

His other claim to fame was in using his abbatial right to pardon a felon condemned to the gallows. This did not meet with so much approval.

Dissolution of the Abbey

In the late Middle Ages the monasteries became inefficient and declined as centres of religion, charity and learning. Yet their conservatism, status and wealth aroused envy and criticism amongst the Reformers. Henry VIII, his treasury bare but tyranny rampant, seized their property, dissolved the religious houses and sold off much of the real estate.

The King's Abbey did not escape. On May 27th, 1538, the royal commissioners, Sir John Gage and Richard Layton, rode across the Market Green and demanded admission. With them came their servants, 'decked in the spoils of desecrated chapels, with copes for doublets, tunics for saddle cloths and the silver relic-cases hammered into sheaths for their daggers'. Resistance was impossible but, for all the criticism of the Abbey, these New Rich made themselves despised by townsmen as well as brethren. The townsfolk were intensely conservative, they and their forefathers had lived within the shadow of the Abbey for centuries and they respected the Abbot, John Hamond, a native of Battle. The sight of these 'furriners' flaunting their ill-gotten gains was too much for their way of thinking.

According to the commissioners, however, they gained little from Battle Abbey. They wrote to Secretary Thomas Cromwell protesting about 'the implements of the household ... the worst that ever I saw in Abbey or Priory'. This begs the question as to how much Abbey treasure had been disposed of, how much spirited away by Abbot and brethren or their predecessors, and how much purloined for themselves. Another letter of this time gives a list of the commission's plunder:– of copes, two blue 'rousty and soylled', one green embroidered and one crimson velvet; 'If you will have any of these send me worde. The best vestment I can fynde ye shall have but I assure you so many evill I never see'. At least one treasure survives – the Battle Abbey sword (wielded by the Warrior Abbot?) was taken by Sir John Gage and remained with his decendants until presented to the armoury at Goodrich Court.

The Abbey itself was doomed. The commissioners broke the Abbey seals and on July 6th, 1538, the Abbot, the Prior and sixteen brethren were dismissed on pensions, Abbot John Hamond retiring to live in Upper Lake (between the Abbey north wall and the Parish Church). The 'plate and jewels' were reserved for the King, 'the furniture and goods' sold, what money there was sent to the Augmentation Office and the muniments, including the royal charters, retained for the new landlord. Of the buildings left standing, the Abbot's House was also retained for the landlord, Sir Anthony Browne, a favourite of the King. Sir Anthony laid out his garden on the site of the Abbey Church.

 The destruction of the Abbey took less than three months and the demolisher was 'one Gilmer'. The foundation of the Conqueror, magnified over the centuries, was suddenly and tragically no longer.

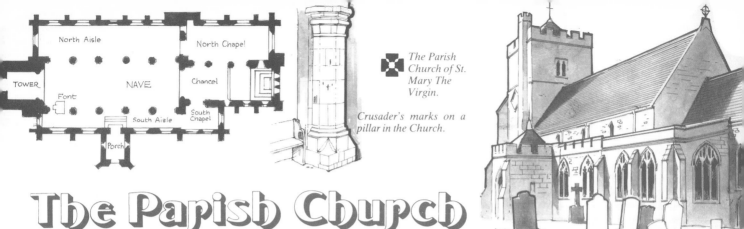

The Parish Church of St. Mary The Virgin.

Crusader's marks on a pillar in the Church.

The Parish Church

The original townsmen who erected the first Abbey buildings attended the Abbey Church. But this was contrary to the Benedictine Order and, as the parishioners multiplied, they overcrowded the Abbey Church and offended the monks. The monks therefore built outside the Abbey walls 'a chapel in honour of the Blessed Mother of God in which a priest might, under the direction of the Abbot or the brethren, serve the parishioners'. Thus the Parish Church came under the wing of the Abbey and benefited from its privileges. From the earliest times the monk who came across the road to take the services was known as the Dean, a title inherited by the parish priest to the present.

The first small Church was built by Abbot Ralph (1107) but very little of this remains. The body of the existing Church was built about 1230, enlarged about 1450 and restored internally in the 19th century by Butterfield. The font of Purbeck marble is Norman and its wooden cover one of the most ancient in Sussex. A fragment of old glass surviving shows a saintly archbishop, perhaps St. Thomas à Becket who, as Chancellor, had supported Abbot Walter. During the Civil War indignant Puritans paraded through the Church despoiling colourful ornaments.

The outstanding monument is the alabaster tomb of Sir Anthony Browne and his first wife, Alis.

An outstanding parishioner was Isaac Ingall who served the Church till well over ninety, objected to being retired and died at 120. His grave is beyond the east end of the Church. Beyond the west end lie John and Martha Lansdell, who died on the 8th June 1818, aged one day.

An illustrated guide, 'St. Mary the Virgin, Battle, Sussex', can be bought inside the Church.

Sir Anthony Browne taken from his effigy in the Church of St. Mary the Virgin, Battle. The tomb is the work of a student of Michael Angelo.

'...to the Said Anthony Browne Forever'

Sir Anthony Browne and his successors, who were granted the holdings and rights of the Abbey forever, were devout Papists. But, though Sir Anthony held to the old faith, the monks regarded the Abbey's destruction and their expulsion as sacrilege. These transgressions called for eternal damnation and eternally damned the Brownes were – in dramatic fashion.

The scene is the surviving great hall, the occasion a banquet to celebrate the Browne occupation. Suddenly the massive doors swing open, as if by supernatural force. One of the ejected monks appears taper in hand, features waxen. There is a momentary silence at the apparition, then the diners ignore his presence – courtly, disdainful, jesting. But the monk strides ominously to the high table, inflinching, forbidding. He thunders forth his curse, commanding attention: "Mark ye, my masters, ye that take God's holy land ... for your own carnal purposes. God's curse shall be upon ye and your name shall be wiped out of the land by fire and water". His blazing eyes never leave Sir Anthony's until he is finished. The monk has made his impact; the aftermath is dismay and alarm, the scornful jests now of bravado.

The Curse of Battle Abbey, a well-known legend, was not apparently fulfilled until much later. In 1793 Cowdray House, then the Browne seat, was destroyed by fire, and about the same time the last Browne, Viscount Montague, was drowned trying to shoot some rapids on the Rhine. His sister's children were also drowned at Bognor in 1815, and in 1931 there was a disastrous fire at the Abbey.

Sir Anthony died in 1548, long outlived by his second wife, 'the fair Geraldine', immortalised by the poet Surrey. His manor house, completed by his son, the first Viscount Montague, is still known as Princess Elizabeth's Lodging as this was intended for the education of the future Elizabeth I. Viscount Montague represented Mary I ('Bloody Mary') in Rome but he also proved himself loyal to the Protestant Elizabeth. When England was threatened by the Spanish Armada 'the first to show his Bands to the Queen was that noble, virtuous … Viscount Montague'. His successor, with four country houses to upkeep, fell into debt, and during the Civil War the Royalist Montagues lost 300 acres of Battle Great Park. The Restoration hardly improved their fortunes. The fifth Viscount, a supporter of James II, ousted in the Glorious Revolution, pulled down the Abbey kitchens and sold the materials. Finally the sixth Viscount sold the Abbey itself. Cowdray had long been the chief family seat, and the Abbey was becoming dilapidated and haunted by smugglers.

The 'Fair Geraldine'.

Sir Thomas Webster
Sir Whistler Webster
Sir Godfrey Vassal Webster Bart
Lord Byron

Hosts of Society

FIDES · ET · JUSTITIA

The arms of the Websters

The new owner in 1719 was Sir Thomas Webster, the first Baronet, one of whose ancestors had been master cook to Elizabeth I. Sir Thomas was a man of great wealth, some of which came to him with his wife, the heiress of Henry Whistler, M.P. for Oxford, 1623-'40. He had considerable property in London and also bought Bodiam Castle, Robertsbridge Abbey and houses at Fairlight. His son, Sir Whistler Webster, re-organized the estate but the property appears to have declined further during the eighteenth Century. The fourth Baronet, Sir Godfrey Webster, married at thirty-eight Elizabeth Vassal (15), while he was Governor of Jamaica. Ten years later in Italy she met Lord Holland and eloped with him. As Lady Holland, she presided over one of the great salons of the regency, entertaining such luminaries as Lord Byron.

Her son, Sir Godfrey Vassal Webster, spent huge sums improving the property. But he was a notorious gambler, even for those days of high stakes, and by 1825 he was ruined. He had to sell not only £90,000 of timber and the Bodiam, Robertsbridge and Fairlight properties, but a unique collection of Abbey deeds and documents. He received a miserable price for these muniments, which are now in the Huntington Library, California. In 1858, Sir Augustus Webster, the seventh baronet. sold the property to the future Duke of Cleveland. The reign of his duchess is still remembered. She too became a famous hostess, though a more stately one than the artistic Lady Holland. A close friend of her's was Lord Kitchener of Khartoum. He sent her a white donkey which she used to ride up the High Street, followed by a self-conscious flunkey on a brown one.

Sir Augustus Webster, the eighth baronet, bought back the Abbey for his family in 1901. It remained in the family until 1976 when it was taken over by the Department of the Environment. More recently English Heritage have become custodians of the monument. For over 60 years the buildings were let to a girls' boarding school which recently became co-educational.

The Duke of Cleveland

The Duchess of Cleveland

37

Battle over Nine Centuries

High Street 1909

Townlife revolved around the Abbey from its foundation to the Dissolution. As a 'royal peculiar' the Abbey became one of the most influential religious establishments. It owned large estates throughout southern England and held the patronage of more than fifty churches, as well as being independent. With this background the Town naturally developed into the agricultural and civil centre of the countryside, besides being its religious authority. The Abbey archives record that cattle, poultry and farm produce were regularly brought into the Town from the Abbey manors as far afield as Wye in Kent and Alciston in Sussex. The Town also became a collection centre for the export of wool, with "Many specialists of luxury articles … attracted to Battle by virtue of the abbey …"*.

From the Abbey archives it is clear that the Abbot held extensive legal powers through his manorial courts.

Battle did not stop being the local metropolis when the lay owners took over the Abbey. For many years after the Dissolution it continued as a religious centre, for the Papist Montagues made it the Roman Catholic headquarters of the area. During his visitation in 1569, the Archbishop of Canterbury found Battle to be 'the most Popish

* References: "Bygone Battle" and "Lordship and Community".

38

town in all Sussex'. The Town also remained a farming market and, in due course, it became the centre of gunpowder, iron and other industries.

Despite its importance as a centre, the population of Battle has grown remarkably slowly. 'The Chronicle of Battel Abbey' recorded 115 private holdings in 1100 but, as recently as 1924, there were about the same number. In 1150 the population was approximately 750-1000, yet six centuries later it had only risen to about 1500. By 1801, the first census year when there were troops in barracks, it was 2040. In 1851, when the railway was being built, it was 3849 (including the railway workers). By 1921 it was 2891 and, only since the building of houses along the approach roads from 1924 onwards has it again exceeded the 3000 mark. In 1991 (the last census) it had risen to 5569.

The Pilgrims' Rest

Over the past few centuries, the shape of central Battle and its architecture have not changed much either. A 17th century inhabitant returning to the Town would have little difficulty finding his way from the windmill on Caldbec Hill to the Parish Church. Yet Battle has always been a practical place, trying to keep abreast of time, replacing old features with modern equivalents. In the 17th-18th centuries there was a good deal of tiling and stucco work on the half-timbered, still solid fronts of the houses. In fact the framework of the various old buildings in the Town centre has remained largely intact; only the façades have been updated. A plate glass window, a stucco or modern brick front probably conceals the original timber and brick building, which is easily visible from the back of the house. Not that any of the houses are the original dwellings of the 11th-12th centuries. Nothing material remains to give an idea of how the primitive townsfolk lived.

39

Houses of Interest

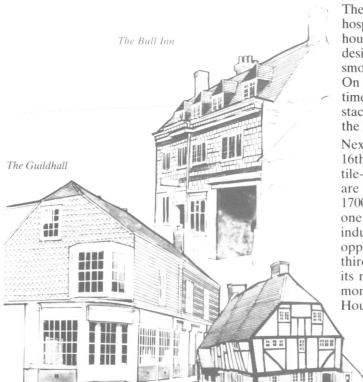

The Bull Inn

The Guildhall

The Crooked House (Lewinscroft)

The Pilgrims' Rest, rebuilt on the site of a 12th century hospitium (guest quarters) about 1420, is a timber-framed house below the Abbey Gateway. Its central hall, designed like those of the barons, has a great hearth, the smoke from which drifted up through a hole in the roof. On each side is a two-storied wing, modified at various times, and above the tiled roof is a 16th century chimney stack. Wayfarers have been guests here during and since the Middle Ages.

Next to the Pilgrims' Rest and throughout inner Battle are 16th-17th century cottages, originally half-timbered, now tile-hung with overlapping upper floors. Set amongst them are grander houses, many of which were renewed about 1700 for the traders, artisans, lesser gentry and possibly one or two of the iron-masters who thrived during Battle's industrial age (of which more shortly). One such building, opposite the Pilgrims' Rest, is Langton House with its third storey and balcony added around this date. It takes its name from the Langton family, the last of whom left money for the Town's first charity school. Inside Langton House is the Battle Museum.

Going up the High Street from the Abbey it is easy to evoke the King's Highway of the 18th century. The still rough and rutted road is used by coaches, the odd carriage, waggons and horses; traffic is often halted by farm animals being driven to market, by mud, refuse and pot holes in the track. Alongside, local society chatters freely and jovially. The gentry, wealthier farmers and traders wear tricorn hats, plain cloaks, breeches and stockings, buckled shoes or high boots. Their ladies in little muslin caps, floral bonnets or feminine tricorns hold their skirts over the unpaved side-walks.

Today people are busier, have less time for chatter, yet the atmosphere, the history, remain. There are several houses of particular interest, mostly on the left of the High Street (facing west). Until its recent closure, William Till's at Number 19 (now Clements, soft furnishings) was said to be the oldest ironmongers in the kingdom. It was opened by Master John Hammond in 1680 and its early customers included: 'my Lord Ashburnham, the Honbl. Lord Montague, Sir Thomas Webster'. Number 22, just above Clements, is the Old Pharmacy, a Tudor building dated 1500. It has an 18th century bow window which blends nicely with the blackened beams and whitened plaster. Almost opposite (59 - 60) is Saffron Picture Gallery, similar in style but rather older with 15th century ceiling beams. Again on the left at Number 27 is the Bull Inn, built in 1688 from the stone of the Abbey kitchens on the site of the medieval "Bull". At the top of the High Street is the Almonry which was erected on land set aside for the Abbey

Almoner. The main stone block is 15th century and the interior contains good examples of the 16th-17th century craftsmanship. Number 24, opposite the turning into Mount Street, is a 16th century house known as the Guildhall, partly built over the cellar of what was thought to be the original (Claverham) guildhall.

Up Mount Street on the right is the "Crooked House". This lath and plaster building, with its overhanging upper storey and acute angles, is an accumulation of different periods.

Returning down Mount Street and the High Street brings one to Upper Lake. Below the Parish Church on the left is the Prior's Lodge which dates back to the 12th century. This is where the last Abbot retired after the Dissolution.

The Deanery, behind the Church, is a noble Tudor house of mellowed red brick and stone facings. It was a large vicarage (now a private house) for the parish, befitting the regal history of the place.

The Deanery

Awaiting Napoleon

From the 16th to the 19th centuries Battle reverted to its origins as a place of war. During this period it was in the iron (gun) foundry country and the centre of the gunpowder industry. At the turn of the 18th century a garrison was stationed in Battle to resist Napoleon.

' …. only 200 years ago East Sussex was the Black Country of Britain … the skies glowed at night from the glare of the furnaces and the valleys reverberated to the clang of the trip hammers'. The newly-rich iron masters, who traded with and possibly lived in Battle, found this area ideally suitable. The requirements for the smelting and transport of iron were present in quantity – deposits of iron ore in the Wealden clay, a still-vast forest for the charcoal and the nearness of tidal estuaries in the absence of good roads. In Tudor times water power was developed for driving the water wheels. These worked the bellows at the furnaces and trip hammers at the forges, where the cast iron was wrought into shape.

The most important products at the furnaces were the guns. The first iron cannon was cast in 1543 at Buxted, less than twenty miles from Battle, and cannon for the English fleet which defeated the Spanish Armada came from this area. Cannon were not only bought for the armed forces; there was a lucrative trade in smuggling them abroad. The most widely sold of the products, however, were the iron fire backs. One of these, embossed ER (Elizabeth Regina), was on display at the Abbey for many years, and there are others still to be seen in or around Battle.

As coal superseded charcoal in the eighteenth century Battle became famous for its gunpowder. According to Daniel Defoe, author of "Robinson Crusoe", Battle was 'remarkable for making the finest gunpowder ... in Europe'. The "English Encyclopaedia" of 1809, listing the regulations for gunpowder manufacture, states that 'only 40 pounds of powder is to be made at one time under one pair of stones, except Battle powder ...' At Peppering-eye in 1676 four parcels of brook land were let to John Hammond (the first ironmonger) with permission to erect a powder mill. Eventually Park Mill, now Powdermill House, became the chief of seven mills in Battle when the industry was at its most prosperous. The manufacture lasted through the Napoleonic and Crimean Wars until 1876, when the Duke of Cleveland refused to renew the licenses of the mills as the frequent explosions were destroying the Duchess's nerves. The Napoleonic period was also the heyday of smuggling, and opportunities were not missed of exchanging the gunpowder for smuggled brandy. The memory of Battle powder lived until recently with the manufacture of a famous firework, the "Battle Rouser".

During the invasion scares of the Napoleonic wars, a first reserve battalion was quartered in Battle. A barracks was built for the soldiers on the east side of the Whatlington Road, of which only Barrack Cottage, without its weather-boarding, remains.

The Volunteers (Home Guard), from professors to rustics, drilled with their pikes on Market Green. Ladies besported military fashions and offered romantic diversions. Preparations were made for evacuation by farm waggons. Patriotism was the order of the day as rumours circulated: the French were making a bridge across the Channel, then it was a tunnel; they were coming in huge balloons; Bonaparte was here already, in disguise. Occasionally there was time-off from the training, the preparations. In 1798, Prince William of Gloucester ('Silly Billy') was brought from Hastings to visit Battle's oldest parishioner, Isaac Ingall. He was given a gold sovereign and a pinch of snuff. Eight days later he died, aged 120.

And for all the excitement, the Battle of Britain spirit, 'Boney' never came.

Preaching Revolution

In the depression after the Napoleonic Wars, peasant protest spread quickly and chaotically through the southern counties. The peasants carried no arms and little blood was shed, but occasionally a harsh workhouse overseer was ducked in the village pond or paraded in a dung cart. Their action against property was more effective. Barns and ricks were burnt, farm machinery destroyed and workhouses wrecked if their demands were not met. Small farmers and some of the gentry were sympathetic and in the first few weeks of this 'Rural War' mild sentences were passed. Mr. Collingwood, a J.P. of Battle, was officially reprimanded for his leniency.

During this period, when the Royal Mail coach was running from the George Hotel (High Street) to London in record time, William Cobbett, the agitator, was 'stumping' into Battle on one of his "Rural Rides". He did not, in fact, advocate bloody revolution but warned of the revolts that would follow if nothing was done. On October 16th, 1830, he spoke from a booth to a meeting in Battle. He roused his audience to alternate bursts of applause, laughter and extreme anger. He condemned the burning and destruction but welcomed the increases in wages which resulted. He finished: 'Here is a petition ready, let us all sign it; and then we shall soon be restored to the happy state in which our forefathers lived'.

In his "Political Register" he wrote: 'At Battle last night ... a stage made with faggots and boards, for me to stand on; a small table with two candles on it before me; a chair for me to sit on before I began; an audience consisting of about 500 persons, chiefly from the villages around the town ... about a third part of the audience in smock frocks; about a twentieth part of it consisting of women, mostly young; and, while the rest of the auditory had to stand all the while, seats had been provided for a row of these pretty Sussex women (always admired by me), who were thus ranged directly before me! I was really at home here: here were assembled a sample of that part of the honest, sincere, kind and once free and happy people, amongst whom I was born and bred up, and towards whom my affections have increased with my age'.

A week or two later fires were roaring in the district and Battle became one of the riot-centres of the campaign. Two Battle labourers, a man named Bushby and Thomas Goodwin, a cooper, were sentenced to death for arson. The authorities made efforts to implicate Cobbett in the rising, and Goodwin signed a statement blaming Cobbett's lectures for causing it. He was pardoned and hustled from the country, but Bushby was hanged. Despite support from the farmers, labourers and craftsmen of Battle, Cobbett was accused by the government of inciting labourers to violence. But the proceedings developed into a trial of the government rather than of Cobbett, the jury disagreed on a verdict and the revolutionary was freed.

 William Cobbett, farmer and countrylover, author of "Rural Rides" and "Cottage Industry", critic of 'whiskered gentry' and Tory MP's out of touch with tenants. He admired the French Revolution yet agitated for a return to old values, Identified with the yeoman of England, deploring the loss of peasant independence. His horse-plodding through Sussex was done in wet weather; he was often soaked to the skin, torn by coughing, scarcely eating.
Peasant smocks (see Battle Museum) caricatured in Cartoons and Victorian jokes. Battle peasants were very conservative but low wages, high prices and local encouragement provoked some to rioting and destruction.

A Little England

The title above is not to suggest that Battle is a little town isolated by its countryside and its history – rather the opposite. Its history and to an extent its countryside have made it unique, a little England that gave rise to a great nation. It is a little England that has always possessed those qualities which have made England herself great. The people of Battle do not simply inherit the independence and conservatism that characterise the sturdy Sussex yeoman. They display something more than this – the self-confidence, the enterprise and sense of justice that make them almost more than 'mere English'.*

From the beginning they have held to their values, the values that outlast time and change. Two quotations from the "Chronicle of Battel Abbey" illustrate the contention: 'Likewise at the labour of the meadows or the mill, if it shall be necessary to go thither more than is just, they may not be compelled, yet being entreated, they shall go if able' ... 'The men of this town, on account of the very great dignity of the place, are called Burgesses'. The demise of the Abbey did not abate their enterprise or sense of values. Battle was always the centre of something, it was always individual. Apart from the 'Popery', the gunpowder mills, the continuing market, the characters who were the Abbey owners, there was for example a long-established clockmaking industry, a thriving tannery, a shoe factory run by the Thorpe family. Celebrated authors such as Warwick Deeping and Sheila Kaye-Smith have lived in Battle.

Elizabeth I about herself.

Above all, Battle is a town of honest, liberal people. There is a spirit of community here which rarely exists elsewhere, a spirit of helpfulness for all the wariness of the 'furriner'. No-one could have expressed the spirit of this 'Place of Battel' better than William Cobbett when he wrote, 'I was really at home here'.

'Although here the English ... accepted conquest and bowed in a new destiny, yet ever must the name of Harold be honoured in the Island for which he and his famous Housecarles fought indomitably to the end'.

Sir Winston Churchill "A History of the English-speaking Peoples" Vol. I.

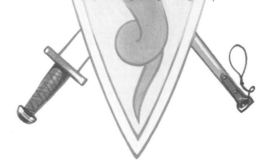